WELCOME TO THE U.S.A.

ALABAMA

Written by Ann Heinrichs   Illustrated by Matt Kania
Content Adviser: Gregory Michael Dorr, PhD, Assistant Professor
of History, University of Alabama, Tuscaloosa, Alabama

The Child's World

Published in the United States of America by The Child's World®
PO Box 326 • Chanhassen, MN 55317-0326
800-599-READ • www.childsworld.com

Photo Credits

Cover: Getty Images/Digital Vision; frontispiece: William A. Bake/Corbis.

Interior: Dan Brothers/Alabama Bureau of Tourism and Travel: 30; Ted Bryson/Colbert County Tourism & Convention Bureau; Corbis: 28 (Reuters), 29 (Raymond Gehman); Fort Payne/DeKalb County Tourist Association: 6; Getty Images: 25, (Hulton|Archive), 26 (Stone/Andy Sacks); J. Scott Howell/Robinson Iron Corp.: 21, 22; Library of Congress: 11; Mobile Bay CVB: 33; Moundville Archaeological Park, The University of Alabama: 13; National Oceanic and Atmospheric Administration/National Estuarine Research Reserve Collection: 9; National Park Service: 14; Karim Shamsi-Basha/Alabama Bureau of Tourism and Travel: 17, 18; Sipsey Wilderness Hiking Club: 10.

Acknowledgments

The Child's World®: Mary Berendes, Publishing Director

Editorial Directions, Inc.: E. Russell Primm, Editorial Director; Katie Marsico, Associate Editor; Judith Shiffer, Assistant Editor; Matt Messbarger, Editorial Assistant; Susan Hindman, Copy Editor; Melissa McDaniel, Proofreader; Peter Garnham, Matt Messbarger, Olivia Nellums, Chris Simms, Molly Symmonds, Katherine Trickle, Carl Stephen Wender, Fact Checkers; Tim Griffin/IndexServ, Indexer; Cian Loughlin O'Day, Photo Researcher and Editor

The Design Lab: Kathleen Petelinsek, Design and art production

Library of Congress Cataloging-in-Publication Data

Heinrichs, Ann.
  Alabama / written by Ann Heinrichs ; cartography and illustrations by Matt Kania.
    p. cm. — (Welcome to the U.S.A.)
  Includes index.
  ISBN 1-59296-370-6 (library bound : alk. paper) 1. Alabama—Juvenile literature.
2. Alabama Geography—Juvenile literature. I. Kania, Matt. II. Title. III. Series.
  F326.3.H453 2005
  976.1—dc22   2004026160

Ann Heinrichs is the author of more than 100 books for children and young adults. She has also enjoyed successful careers as a children's book editor and an advertising copywriter. Ann grew up in Fort Smith, Arkansas, and lives in Chicago, Illinois.

About the Author
Ann Heinrichs

Matt Kania loves maps and, as a kid, dreamed of making them. In school he studied geography and cartography, and today he makes maps for a living. Matt's favorite thing about drawing maps is learning about the places they represent. Many of the maps he has created can be found in books, magazines, videos, Web sites, and public places.

About the
Map Illustrator
Matt Kania

On the cover: **Alabama's gulf coast sunsets are unforgettable.**
On page one: **State lawmakers work inside the capitol in Montgomery.**

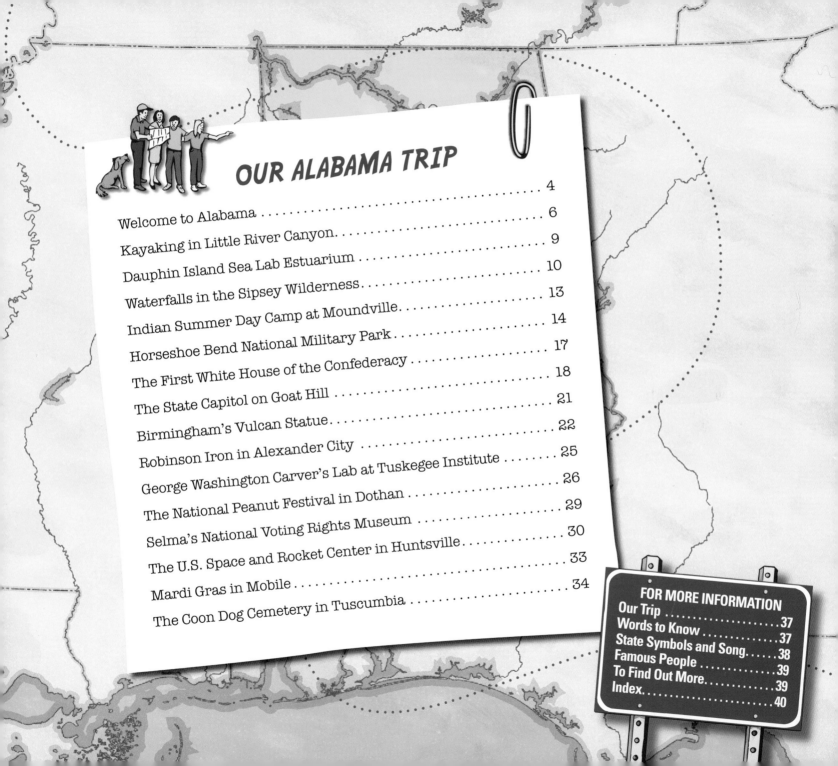

OUR ALABAMA TRIP

Hey! How about a tour through the Heart of Dixie? That's Alabama! You'll climb Goat Hill. You'll meet a coon dog named Troop. You'll hike past waterfalls and take space rides. You'll even see Moon Pies flying through the air! Just follow that loopy dotted line. Or make your own trip by skipping around. Ready? Then buckle up. We're off!

WELCOME TO ALABAMA

As you travel through Alabama, watch for all the interesting facts along the way.

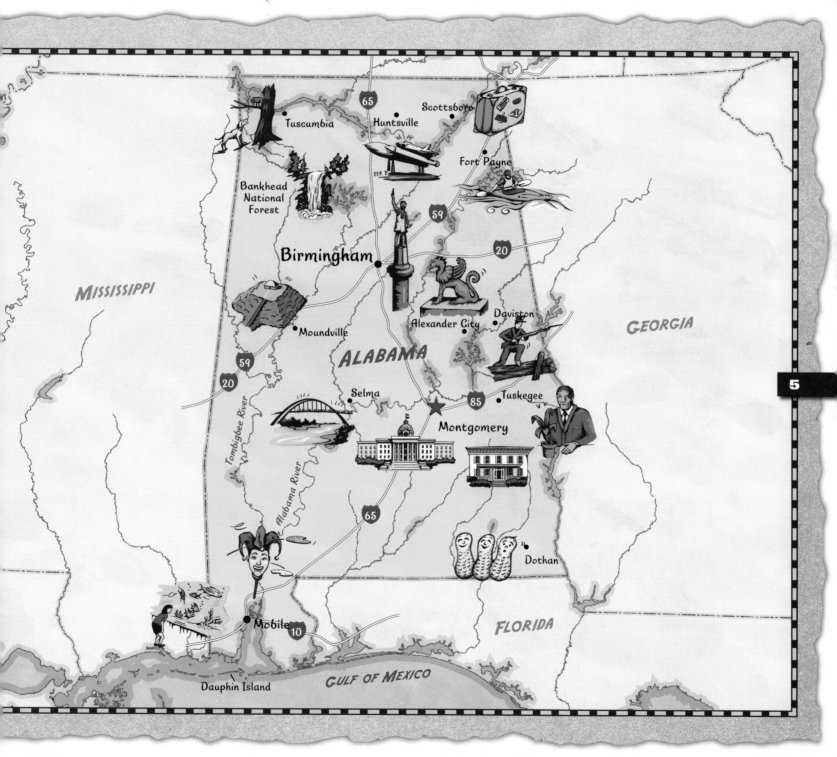

MISSISSIPPI

Tuscumbia

Huntsville

Scottsboro

Fort Payne

Bankhead
National
Forest

65

59

20

Birmingham

ALABAMA

Moundville

Alexander City

Daviston

GEORGIA

59

20

Selma

Tombigbee River

Alabama River

85

Tuskegee

Montgomery

65

Dothan

Mobile

10

FLORIDA

Dauphin Island

GULF OF MEXICO

Kayaking in Little River Canyon

Kayakers love the Little River Falls. You can see awesome kayaking action there.

Whee! The **kayak** plunges down the waterfall. Foamy spray is splashing everywhere. What a blast! It's the thundering waterfall in Little River **Canyon** near Fort Payne.

The Little River is in northeastern Alabama. Mountains and hills cover much of the northeast. Rivers cut deep valleys through them.

The rest of Alabama is lower and more level. The southeast is called the Wiregrass Region. Really tough grass used to grow there. Now it's a rich farming area.

The Mobile River **Delta** is in the southwest. It has many swamps and **bayous.** The river empties into Mobile Bay. That's part of the Gulf of Mexico. Lots of sandy beaches lie along the coast.

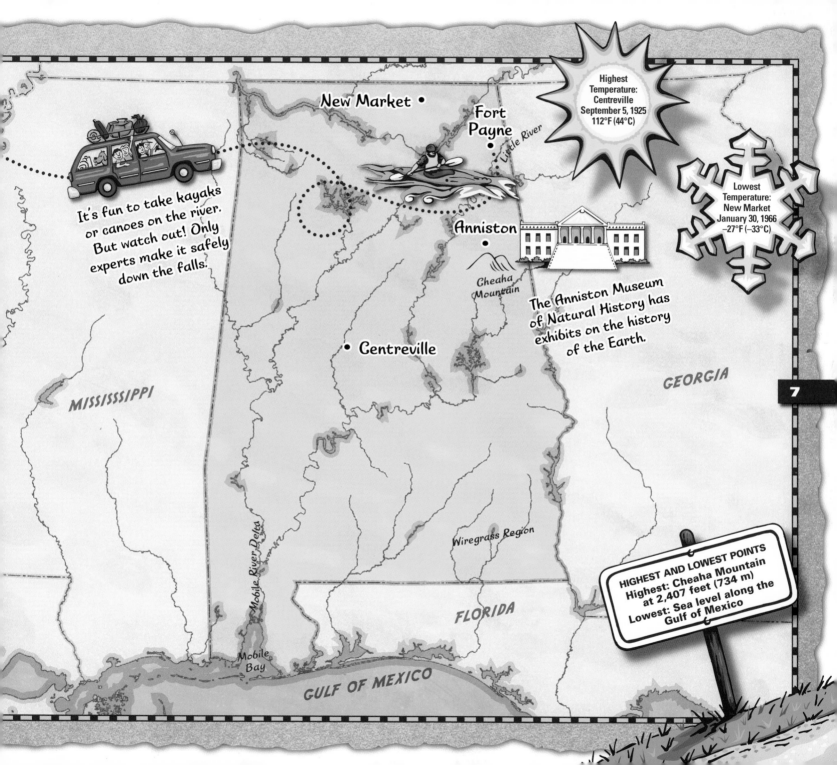

New Market •

Fort Payne •

Little River

It's fun to take kayaks or canoes on the river. But watch out! Only experts make it safely down the falls.

Anniston •

Cheaha Mountain

The Anniston Museum of Natural History has exhibits on the history of the Earth.

• Centreville

MISSISSSIPPI

Mobile River Delta

Wiregrass Region

GEORGIA

FLORIDA

Mobile Bay

GULF OF MEXICO

HIGHEST AND LOWEST POINTS
Highest: Cheaha Mountain at 2,407 feet (734 m)
Lowest: Sea level along the Gulf of Mexico

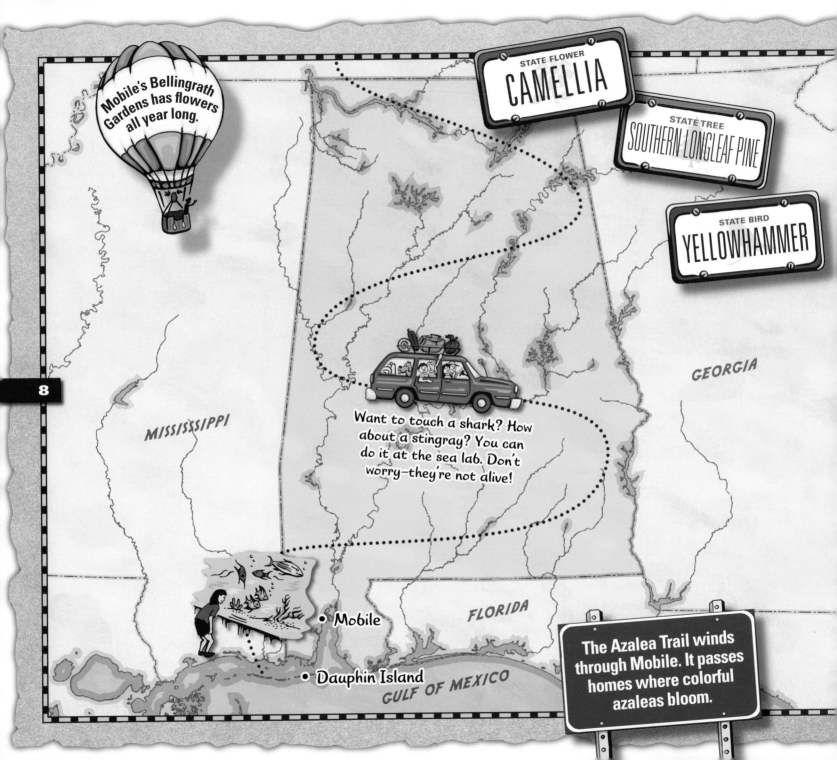

Mobile's Bellingrath Gardens has flowers all year long.

STATE FLOWER
CAMELLIA

STATE TREE
SOUTHERN LONGLEAF PINE

STATE BIRD
YELLOWHAMMER

8

Want to touch a shark? How about a stingray? You can do it at the sea lab. Don't worry—they're not alive!

GEORGIA

MISSISSIPPI

FLORIDA

• Mobile

• Dauphin Island

GULF OF MEXICO

The Azalea Trail winds through Mobile. It passes homes where colorful azaleas bloom.

Dauphin Island Sea Lab Estuarium

It's cool. It's wet. It's got a shell and a long tail. And you're holding it in your hands! Eek!

You're at the Dauphin Island Sea Lab Estuarium. You're handling critters in the touch tank. Can you guess what this one is? It's a horseshoe crab!

Dauphin Island is in the Gulf of Mexico. Sea turtles and crabs live around there. Whales and sharks swim out in the gulf.

Alabama is famous for its flowers. Mobile likes to show off its colorful azaleas. Thick pine forests cover much of Alabama. There you'll find bobcats, foxes, rabbits, and deer. Alligators live in the southern swamps.

Check out the ghost crabs along Weeks Bay. Don't let one sneak up on you!

The National Park Service has 8 sites in Alabama.

Hey! Alabama's biggest tree lives in this wilderness. It's more than 500 years old!

Let's see. Three hundred one, three hundred two . . . . You're deep in the Sipsey Wilderness Area. It's in Bankhead National Forest. It's called the land of a thousand waterfalls. But don't try to count them. It's more fun to go hiking!

There's a lot to see and do in Alabama. Some people explore the mountains and forests. Others enjoy museums, music festivals, or sports.

Football is big in Alabama. The Crimson Tide is a popular team. It's from the University of Alabama in Tuscaloosa. Auburn University's Tigers are popular, too.

Splash in the creeks of Sipsey Wilderness Area.
It's the largest wilderness area in the state.

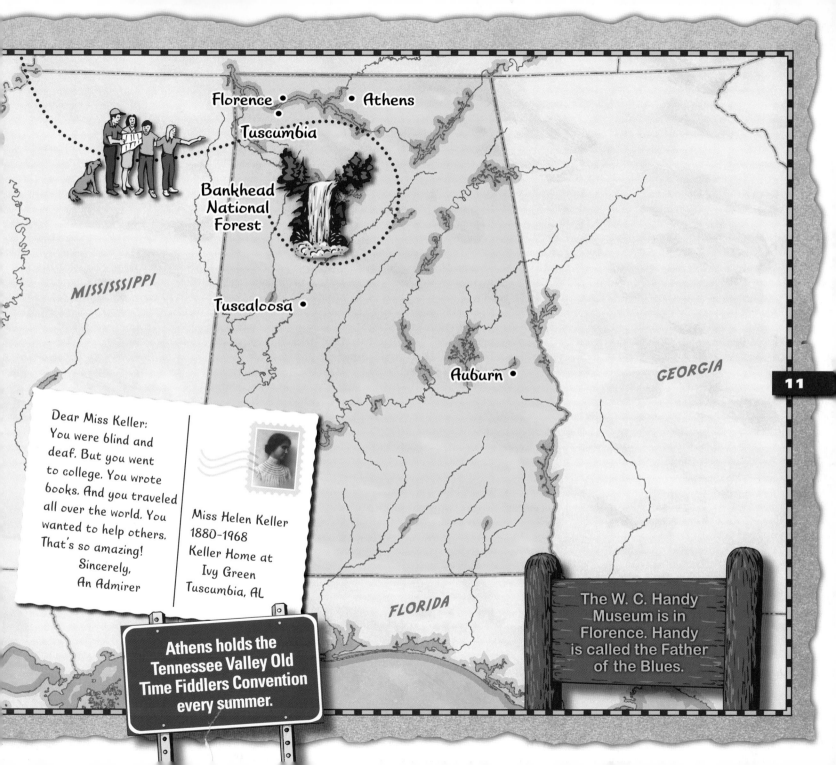

Florence •   • Athens

Tuscumbia •

Bankhead
National
Forest •

MISSISSSIPPI

Tuscaloosa •

Auburn •

GEORGIA

Dear Miss Keller:
You were blind and
deaf. But you went
to college. You wrote
books. And you traveled
all over the world. You
wanted to help others.
That's so amazing!
       Sincerely,
       An Admirer

Miss Helen Keller
1880-1968
Keller Home at
Ivy Green
Tuscumbia, AL

FLORIDA

The W. C. Handy
Museum is in
Florence. Handy
is called the Father
of the Blues.

Athens holds the
Tennessee Valley Old
Time Fiddlers Convention
every summer.

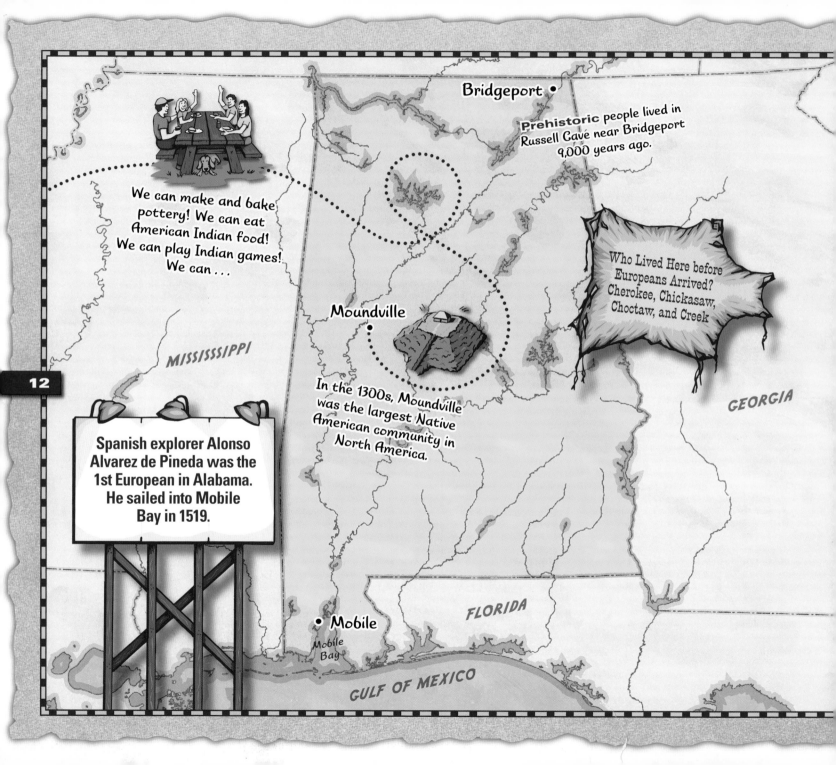

Bridgeport

Prehistoric people lived in Russell Cave near Bridgeport 9,000 years ago.

We can make and bake pottery! We can eat American Indian food! We can play Indian games! We can . . .

Who Lived Here before Europeans Arrived? Cherokee, Chickasaw, Choctaw, and Creek

MISSISSSIPPI

Moundville

In the 1300s, Moundville was the largest Native American community in North America.

GEORGIA

Spanish explorer Alonso Alvarez de Pineda was the 1st European in Alabama. He sailed into Mobile Bay in 1519.

Mobile

Mobile Bay

FLORIDA

GULF OF MEXICO

Indian Summer Day Camp at Moundville

Cut that **gourd** in two. Now, how about making a mask? Cut out eyes and a mouth. Then get some paint and have fun! Red for the eyes. Yellow for the nose. How about blue for the mouth? You're at Indian Summer Day Camp at Moundville!

Native Americans once lived at Moundville. Their city covered hundreds of acres. They built many huge mounds of earth. Some mounds had the leaders' homes on top. Other mounds were graves. The people made pottery and stone and copper goods. Want to learn more about them? Just check out Moundville's museum, classes, and camps.

The mounds at Moundville are huge! Imagine the Indians living here long ago.

In 1540, Hernando de Soto's Spanish troops defeated Chief Tuscaloosa's warriors at Mabila, near present-day Mobile.

Sheesh! This soldier stuff is no picnic.

14

Stand up straight! Chin down, shoulders back! It's 1814. You're a soldier under Andrew Jackson. And you're lined up for a drill. No slouching!

Actually, you're at a program at Horseshoe Bend near Daviston. General Jackson defeated the Creek Indians here. The Creeks had to give up their homeland. It included more than half of present-day Alabama!

Spanish explorers arrived in Alabama in the 1500s. Then white settlers wanted to move in. Little by little, the Native Americans were pushed out.

The Battle of Horseshoe Bend ended the Creek War. Sadly, the Creek Indians lost all their land.

More than 800 Creek Indians died in the Battle of Horseshoe Bend.

The Battle of Horseshoe Bend took place on March 27, 1814.

Daviston

MISSISSSIPPI

Tallapoosa River

GEORGIA

FLORIDA

Alabama was the 22nd state to enter the Union. It joined on December 14, 1819.

Horseshoe Bend is a big curve in the Tallapoosa River.

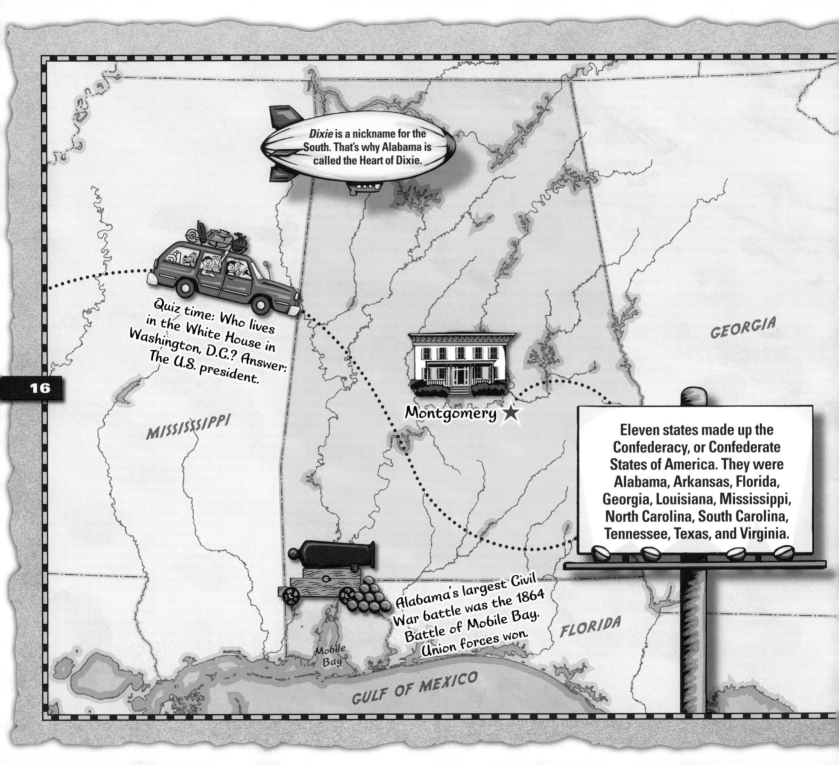

Dixie is a nickname for the South. That's why Alabama is called the Heart of Dixie.

Quiz time: Who lives in the White House in Washington, D.C.? Answer: The U.S. president.

GEORGIA

MISSISSIPPI

Montgomery ★

Eleven states made up the Confederacy, or Confederate States of America. They were Alabama, Arkansas, Florida, Georgia, Louisiana, Mississippi, North Carolina, South Carolina, Tennessee, Texas, and Virginia.

Alabama's largest Civil War battle was the 1864 Battle of Mobile Bay. Union forces won.

Mobile Bay

FLORIDA

GULF OF MEXICO

The First White House of the Confederacy

O kay. It's white. And it's a house. Does that make it the White House? Well, sort of. It's the First White House of the Confederacy. It stands in Montgomery, the first capital of the Confederacy.

The Confederacy was made up of several Southern states. They formed their own nation in 1861. The Confederacy fought the Union, or Northern states, over slavery. This was called the Civil War (1861–1865).

Much of the South depended on farming. In Alabama, farmers grew cotton on large farms. African American slaves were forced to work on these farms. Most Northerners opposed slavery. In the end, the North won. Then the slaves were freed.

There's a White House in Alabama? Learn about the Confederacy as you tour it.

Jefferson Davis was the Confederate president. He lived in the Confederacy's White House.

In 1847, some people tried to rename Goat Hill. They thought it should be Capitol Hill. It didn't work. It's still Goat Hill!

The State Capitol on Goat Hill

So this is Goat Hill, huh? Where are all the goats? Sorry! They're long gone. Goats used to graze there. Now the state capitol sits on that hill. It's the main state government building in Montgomery.

Alabama has three branches of government. One branch makes the state's laws. It's called the legislature. The governor heads another branch. It carries out the laws. Judges make up the third branch. They decide whether someone broke a law.

So this is where Alabama's laws are made. Imagine all those busy government workers inside!

The Supreme Court Library in Montgomery was created in 1828. It was Alabama's 1st large library.

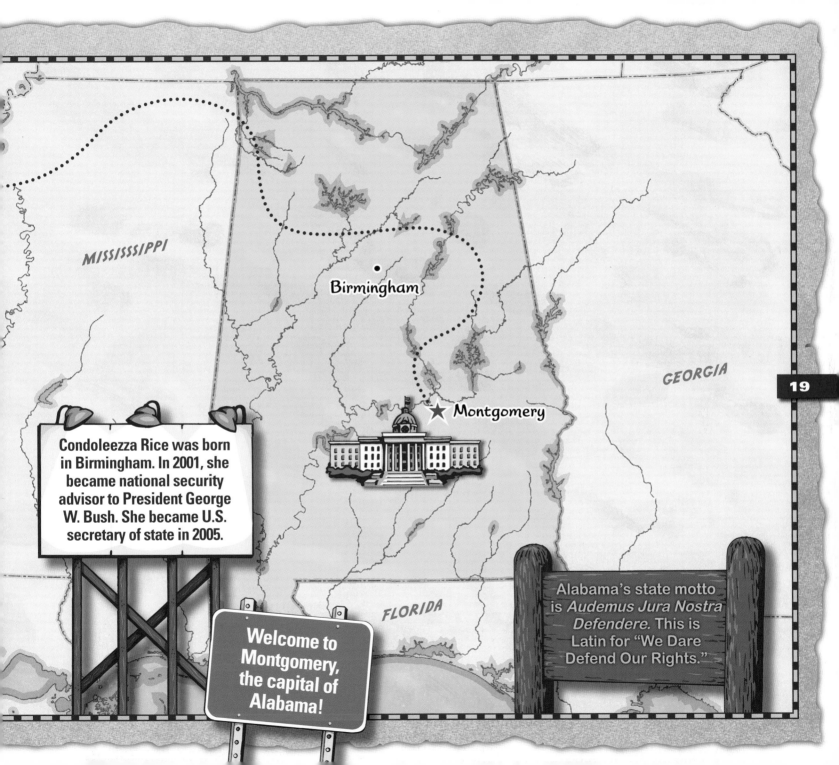

MISSISSIPPI

GEORGIA

Birmingham

★ Montgomery

FLORIDA

Condoleezza Rice was born in Birmingham. In 2001, she became national security advisor to President George W. Bush. She became U.S. secretary of state in 2005.

Welcome to Montgomery, the capital of Alabama!

Alabama's state motto is *Audemus Jura Nostra Defendere.* This is Latin for "We Dare Defend Our Rights."

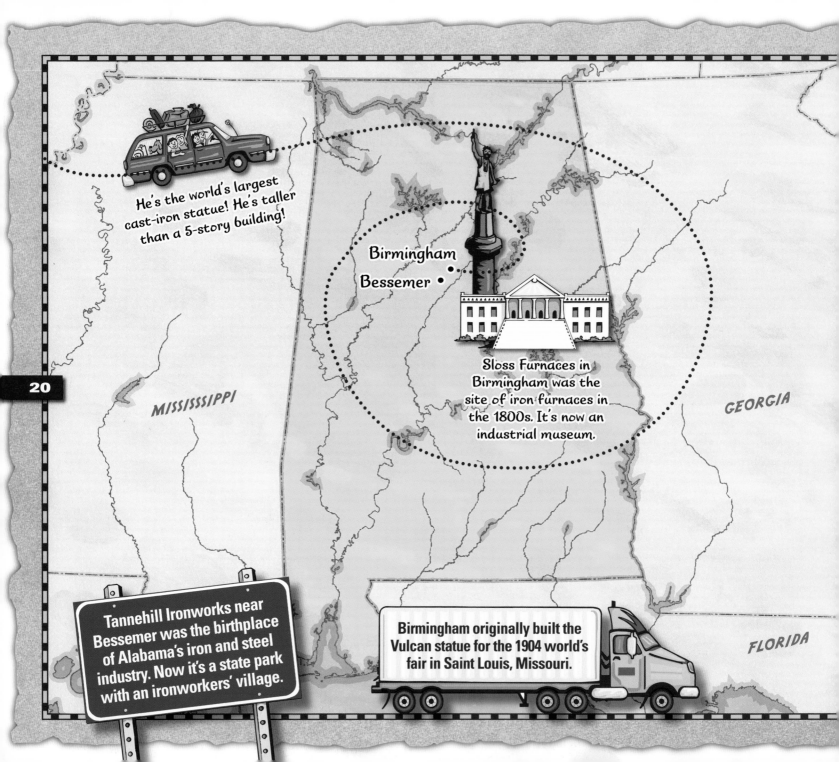

He's the world's largest cast-iron statue! He's taller than a 5-story building!

Birmingham

Bessemer

Sloss Furnaces in Birmingham was the site of iron furnaces in the 1800s. It's now an industrial museum.

MISSISSSIPPI

GEORGIA

FLORIDA

Tannehill Ironworks near Bessemer was the birthplace of Alabama's iron and steel industry. Now it's a state park with an ironworkers' village.

Birmingham originally built the Vulcan statue for the 1904 world's fair in Saint Louis, Missouri.

Birmingham's Vulcan Statue

Hmm. His ears aren't pointy. He doesn't wear a *Star Trek* outfit. And he doesn't say, "Live long and prosper." Is this guy really a Vulcan? He sure is. He's Vulcan himself!

For ancient Romans, Vulcan was the god of fire. They believed he made metals with the fire. So what's his statue doing in Birmingham?

Alabama had many valuable minerals in the 1800s. One was iron. Birmingham began making iron into steel in the 1880s. Fiery furnaces melted the metals. Alabama became a leader in iron and steel. Vulcan stands for these industries. He's got a hammer and a spear point—but no pointy ears!

Vulcan had to be taken down for repair. Now he's back on top where he belongs!

Watch out! There's a big, scary **griffin**! It's half eagle and half lion. Will it attack?

Not this one. You're on a factory tour of Robinson Iron. Workers there make all kinds of iron products. They make fountains, fences, and parts of buildings. And big, scary griffins, too!

Alabama has many busy factories. They make everything from airplane engines to paper bags. Want another fun tour? Visit the Golden Flake snack foods factory in Birmingham. Yum!

22

Robinson Iron has done work for many famous buildings. They're known from New York to China.

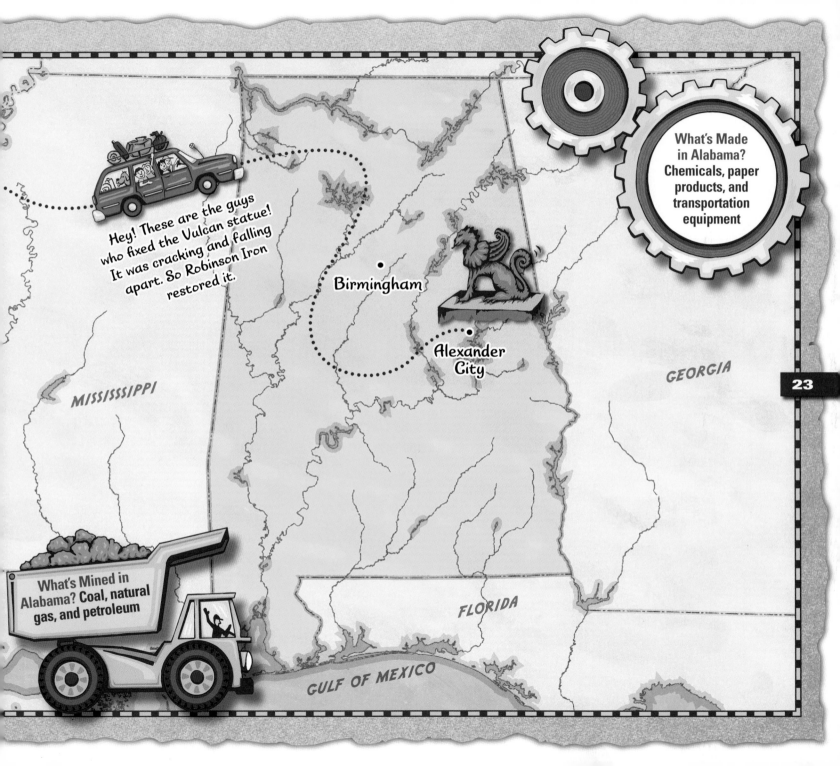

Hey! These are the guys who fixed the Vulcan statue! It was cracking and falling apart. So Robinson Iron restored it.

What's Made in Alabama? Chemicals, paper products, and transportation equipment

MISSISSSIPPI

Birmingham

Alexander City

GEORGIA

What's Mined in Alabama? Coal, natural gas, and petroleum

FLORIDA

GULF OF MEXICO

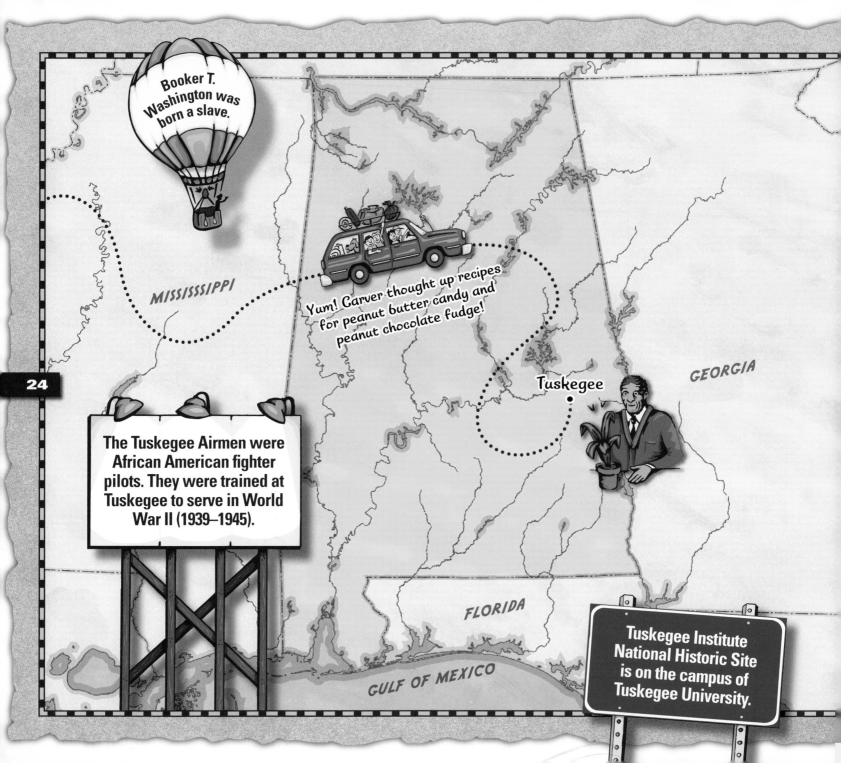

Booker T. Washington was born a slave.

Yum! Carver thought up recipes for peanut butter candy and peanut chocolate fudge!

MISSISSSIPPI

GEORGIA

Tuskegee

The Tuskegee Airmen were African American fighter pilots. They were trained at Tuskegee to serve in World War II (1939–1945).

FLORIDA

GULF OF MEXICO

Tuskegee Institute National Historic Site is on the campus of Tuskegee University.

Microscopes, burners, grinders, and scales. Is this a mad scientist's lab? Nope. It's George Washington Carver's lab at Tuskegee Institute.

Carver was an African American scientist. He had lots of great ideas. He developed better ways to farm. Carver also worked with peanuts and sweet potatoes. He developed hundreds of new products with them.

Booker T. Washington founded Tuskegee Institute in 1881. He opened the school to train African American teachers. He hired Carver and many other fine professors. Today, the school is called Tuskegee University.

Imagine lunches without peanut butter! Thanks, George Washington Carver.

25

Alabama still grows lots of cotton. It's just not the major crop anymore.

The National Peanut Festival in Dothan

So what'll it be? Creamy, crunchy, or extra crunchy? Only one wins the peanut butter grand prize! You're at Dothan's National Peanut Festival. It's the largest peanut festival in the world!

Peanuts are a big deal in the Dothan area. About half the nation's peanuts grow there. But cotton is Alabama's most valuable crop. People called it King Cotton in the 1800s. That's because it ruled the state's **economy.** Now chickens and cattle are the leading farm products. They bring in much more income than cotton.

Alabamans catch shrimp, crabs, and fish, too. Ever heard of a fish farm? Some farmers raise catfish in big ponds.

Do you have arachibutyrophobia? That's the fear of peanut butter sticking to the roof of your mouth!

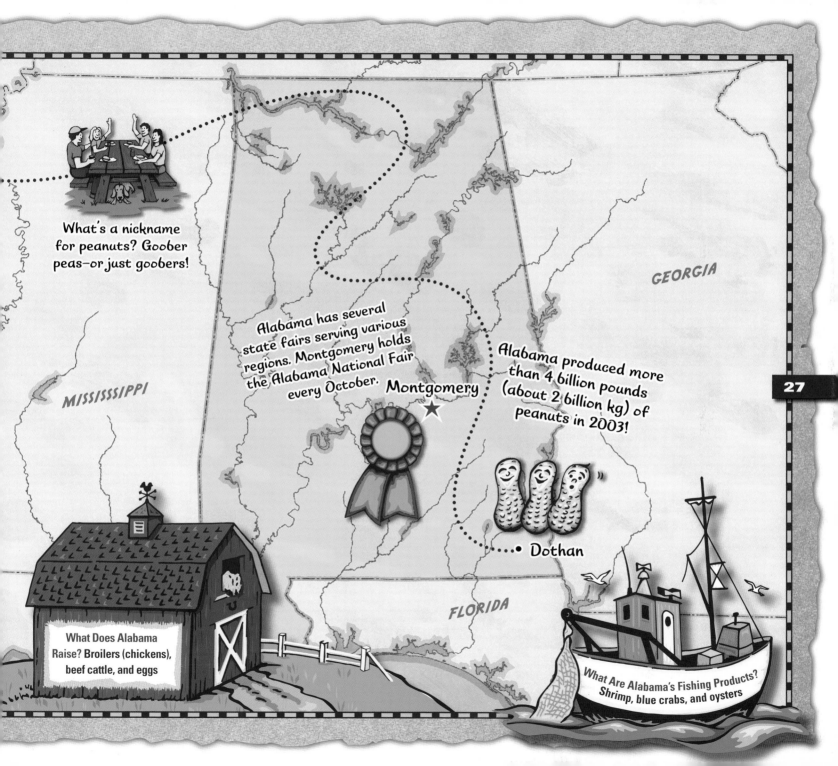

What's a nickname for peanuts? Goober peas—or just goobers!

GEORGIA

MISSISSIPPI

Alabama has several state fairs serving various regions. Montgomery holds the Alabama National Fair every October.

Montgomery

Alabama produced more than 4 billion pounds (about 2 billion kg) of peanuts in 2003!

Dothan

What Does Alabama Raise? Broilers (chickens), beef cattle, and eggs

FLORIDA

What Are Alabama's Fishing Products? Shrimp, blue crabs, and oysters

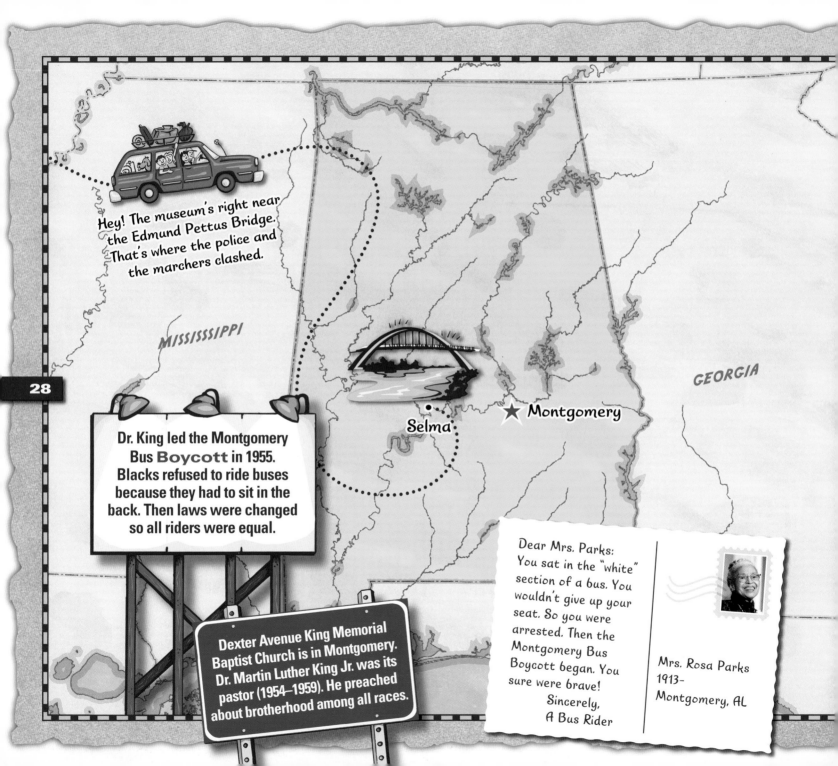

Hey! The museum's right near the Edmund Pettus Bridge. That's where the police and the marchers clashed.

MISSISSSIPPI

GEORGIA

Selma

★ Montgomery

Dr. King led the Montgomery Bus **Boycott** in 1955. Blacks refused to ride buses because they had to sit in the back. Then laws were changed so all riders were equal.

Dexter Avenue King Memorial Baptist Church is in Montgomery. Dr. Martin Luther King Jr. was its pastor (1954–1959). He preached about brotherhood among all races.

Dear Mrs. Parks:
You sat in the "white" section of a bus. You wouldn't give up your seat. So you were arrested. Then the Montgomery Bus Boycott began. You sure were brave!
Sincerely,
A Bus Rider

Mrs. Rosa Parks
1913-
Montgomery, AL

Selma's National Voting Rights Museum

Thousands of people joined the civil rights march from Selma to Montgomery in 1965.

She was just eleven years old. Police on horseback were everywhere. **Tear gas** was burning her eyes. Soon she was thrown in jail. What's going on here?

The year is 1965. The girl is Joanne Bland. She and others were gathered in Selma. They planned to march to Montgomery. They wanted voting rights for African Americans. They hoped Montgomery's lawmakers would support their cause. The Voting Rights Act was passed later that year.

You'll get the whole story in Selma. Just stop by the National Voting Rights Museum. And guess what? Joanne became one of the museum's directors!

Many people fought for civil rights in Alabama. Learn about the their work in Selma.

You're strapped in. You're even weightless for a couple of seconds. Now you know how astronauts feel!

Five, four, three, two, one, liftoff! You shoot up fourteen stories in just a few seconds. Then you free-fall straight down. You're at the U.S. Space and Rocket Center in Huntsville. And you're trying out the wild space rides!

Huntsville is called Rocket City, U.S.A. Space scientists started working there in 1950. They developed many spacecraft. Their rockets helped send astronauts to the Moon. Huntsville is still an important space center.

Huntsville's Space Center is out of this world! The world of space travel comes alive there.

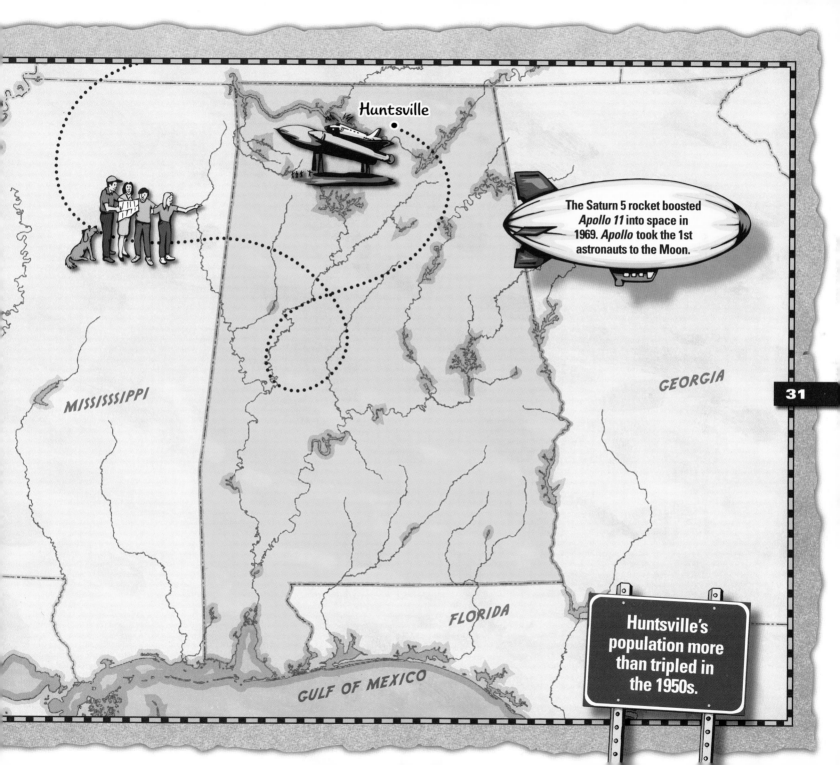

Huntsville

The Saturn 5 rocket boosted *Apollo 11* into space in 1969. *Apollo* took the 1st astronauts to the Moon.

MISSISSSIPPI

GEORGIA

FLORIDA

Huntsville's population more than tripled in the 1950s.

GULF OF MEXICO

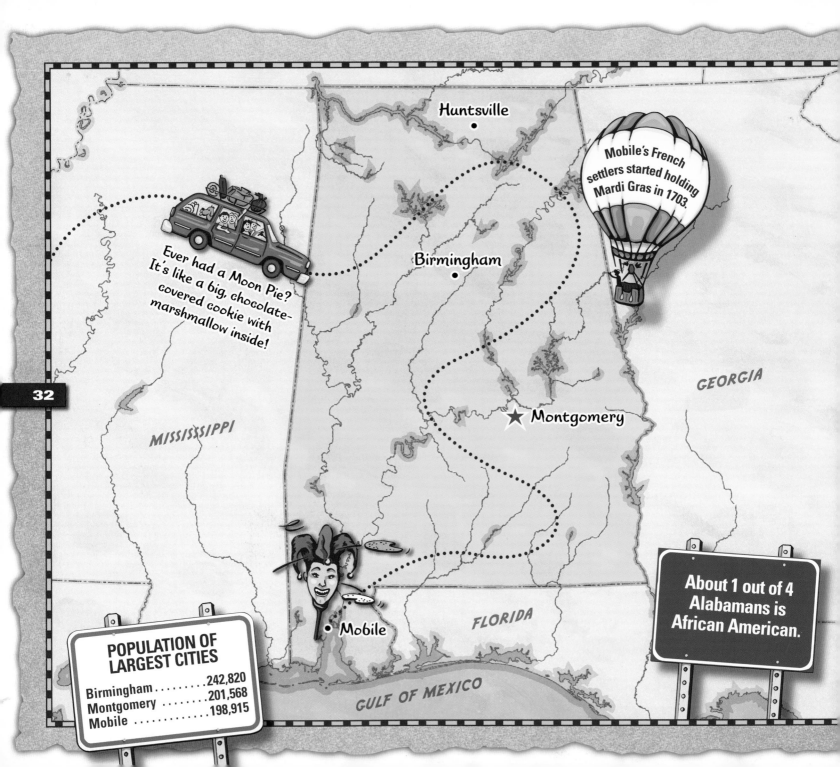

Huntsville

Mobile's French settlers started holding Mardi Gras in 1703.

Ever had a Moon Pie? It's like a big, chocolate-covered cookie with marshmallow inside!

Birmingham

MISSISSIPPI

GEORGIA

★ Montgomery

Mobile

FLORIDA

About 1 out of 4 Alabamans is African American.

POPULATION OF LARGEST CITIES

Birmingham 242,820
Montgomery 201,568
Mobile 198,915

GULF OF MEXICO

Moon Pies are flying through the air! It must be Mardi Gras in Mobile!

Mardi Gras is a big carnival. In Mobile, the fun lasts for two whole weeks. People celebrate with costumes and colorful parades. People toss beads from the parade floats. And some toss Moon Pies, too!

Alabamans have roots all over the world. Just look at Huntsville. More than 100 languages are spoken there!

In 2000, 4,447,100 people lived in Alabama. It's the 23rd-largest state by population.

33

Mobile held America's 1st Mardi Gras. It started in 1703, and people still celebrate!

The Coon Dog Cemetery in Tuscumbia

Maybe it's true that dogs are man's best friend.
Owners sure miss their dogs!

He wasn't fluffy. He wasn't cute. But he sure could hunt. He was Troop, the coon dog. That's a dog that helps hunt raccoons.

Troop was the best darned coon dog ever. His owner thought so, anyhow. He buried Troop in a quiet, grassy place. Now that place is the Coon Dog Cemetery. It's in the little town of Tuscumbia. Almost 200 coon dogs rest there!

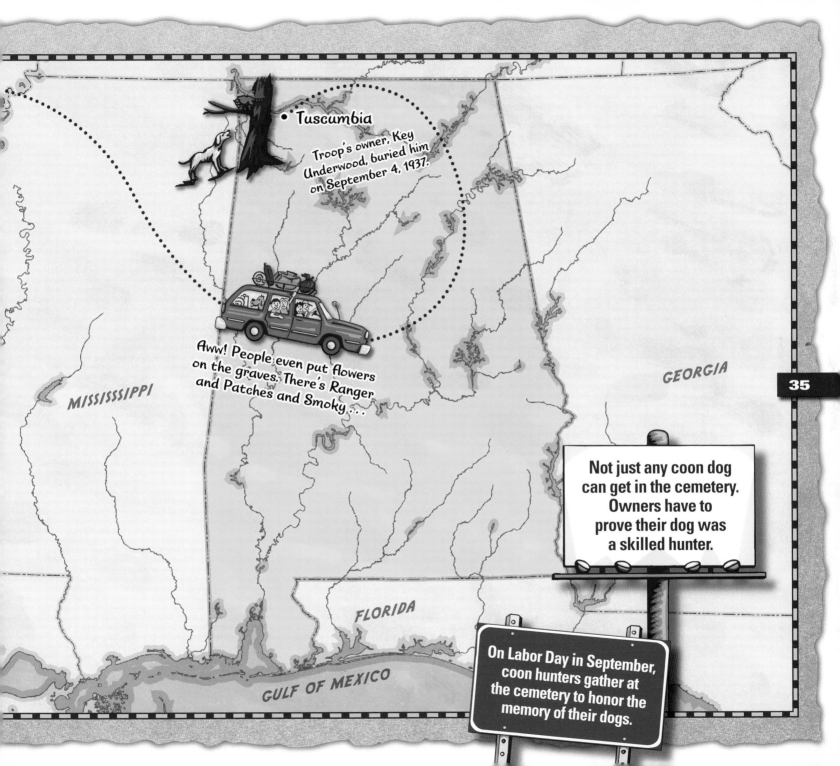

● Tuscumbia

Troop's owner, Key Underwood, buried him on September 4, 1937.

Aww! People even put flowers on the graves. There's Ranger and Patches and Smoky . . .

MISSISSIPPI

GEORGIA

Not just any coon dog can get in the cemetery. Owners have to prove their dog was a skilled hunter.

FLORIDA

GULF OF MEXICO

On Labor Day in September, coon hunters gather at the cemetery to honor the memory of their dogs.

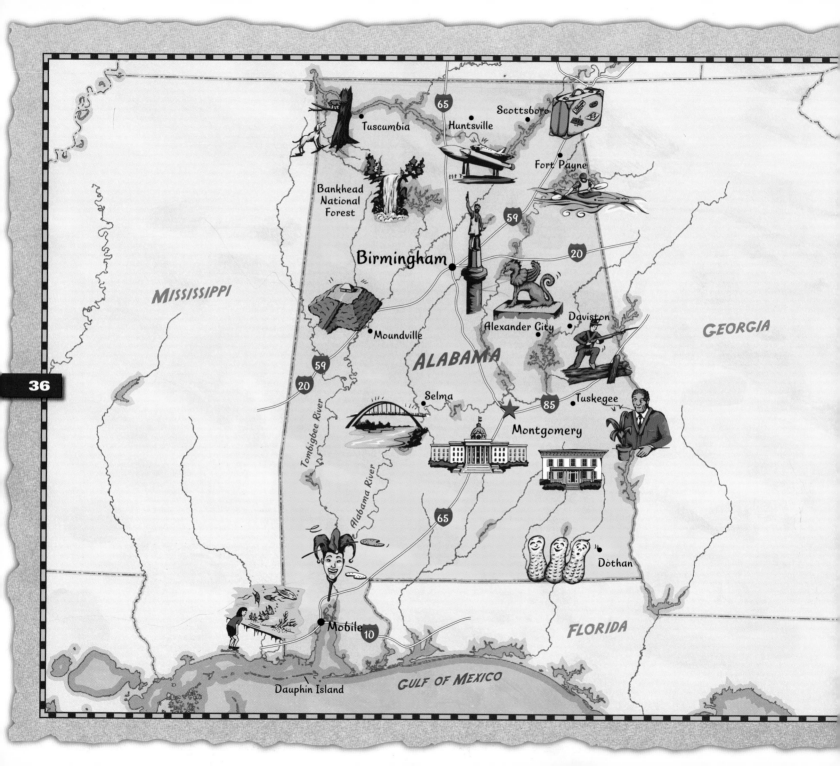

MISSISSIPPI

Tuscumbia

Bankhead
National
Forest

65

Huntsville

Scottsboro

Fort Payne

59

20

Birmingham

Moundville

ALABAMA

Alexander City

Daviston

GEORGIA

59

20

Selma

85

Tuskegee

Montgomery

Tombigbee River

Alabama River

65

65

Mobile

10

Dothan

FLORIDA

Dauphin Island

GULF OF MEXICO

OUR TRIP

We visited many amazing places on our trip! We also met a lot of interesting people along the way. Look at the map on the left. Use your finger to trace all the places we have been.

Where can you see flowers bloom all year long? See page 8 for the answer.

How old is Alabama's biggest tree? Page 10 has the answer.

Who was the 1st European in Alabama? See page 12 for the answer.

How many states made up the Confederacy? Look on page 16 for the answer.

What is arachibutyrophobia? Page 26 has the answer.

How many peanuts were produced in Alabama in 2003? Turn to page 27 for the answer.

What happened at Edmund Pettus Bridge? Look on page 28 and find out!

What are some of the ingredients in a Moon Pie? Turn to page 32 for the answer.

That was a great trip! We have traveled all over Alabama!

There are a few places that we didn't have time for, though. Next time, we plan to visit the Unclaimed Baggage Center in Scottsboro. This store sells unclaimed items that were left at airports. Shoppers can find bargains on everything from books to fancy jewelry!

More Places to Visit in Alabama

WORDS TO KNOW

bayous (BYE-ooz) shallow, slow-moving waterways

boycott (BOI-kot) a protest in which people refuse to buy a company's goods or services

canyon (KAN-yuhn) a deep valley where a river has worn through rock

civil rights (SIV-il RITES) the rights and freedoms of a citizen

delta (DEL-tuh) a triangle-shaped land area at the mouth of a river

economy (i-KON-uh-mee) the activities in a region that make money

gourd (GORD) the hard shell on the outside of a squash or similar plant

griffin (GRI-fuhn) a make-believe beast that's half eagle and half lion

kayak (KYE-ak) a long, narrow boat

prehistoric (pree-hi-STOR-ik) taking place before people began writing down their history

tear gas (TIHR GASS) a harsh gas that stings the eyes, nose, and lungs

Alabama covers 50,744 square miles (131,426 sq km). It's the 28th-largest state in size.

STATE SYMBOLS

State American folk dance: Square dance

State amphibian: Red Hills salamander

State bird: Yellowhammer (flicker)

State flower: Camellia

State fossil: *Basilosaurus cetoides* (zeuglodon)

State freshwater fish: Largemouth bass

State game bird: Wild turkey

State gemstone: Star blue quartz

State horse: Racking horse

State insect: Monarch butterfly

State mascot and butterfly: Eastern tiger swallowtail

State mineral: Hematite (red iron ore)

State nut: Pecan

State reptile: Alabama red-bellied turtle

State rock: Marble

State saltwater fish: Fighting tarpon

State shell: *Scaphella junonia johnstoneae* (Johnstone's junonia)

State soil: Bama soil series

State tree: Southern longleaf pine

State wildflower: Oak-leaf hydrangea

State flag

State seal

STATE SONG

"Alabama"

Words by Julia S. Tutwiler, music by Edna Gockel Gussen

Alabama, Alabama,
We will aye be true to thee,
From thy Southern shore where
   groweth,
By the sea thine orange tree.
To thy Northern vale where floweth
Deep and blue thy Tennessee.
Alabama, Alabama
We will aye be true to thee!

Broad the Stream whose name thou
   bearest;
Grand thy Bigbee rolls along;
Fair thy Coosa-Tallapoosa
Bold thy Warrior, dark and strong.
Goodlier than the land that Moses
Climbed lone Nebo's Mount to see
Alabama, Alabama,
We will aye be true to thee!

From thy prairies broad and fertile,
Where thy snow-white cotton
   shines.
To the hills where coal and iron
Hide in thy exhaustless mines.
Strong-armed miners—sturdy
   farmers:
Loyal hearts what'er we be.
Alabama, Alabama,
We will aye be true to thee!

From the quarries where the marble
White as that of Paros gleams
Waiting till thy sculptor's chisel,

Wake to like thy poet's dream;
For not only wealth of nature,
Wealth of mind hast thou to fee.
Alabama, Alabama,
We will aye be true to thee!

Where the perfumed south-wind
   whispers,
Thy magnolia groves among,
Softer than a mother's kisses
Sweeter than a mother's song;
Where the golden jasmine trailing,
Woos the treasure-laden bee,
Alabama, Alabama,
We will aye be true to thee!

Brave and pure thy men and
   women,
Better this than corn and wine,
Make us worthy, God in Heaven,
Of this goodly land of Thine;
Hearts as open as our doorways,
Liberal hands and spirits free,
Alabama, Alabama,
We will aye be true to thee!

Little, little, can I give thee,
Alabama, mother mine;
But that little—hand, brain, spirit,
All I have and am are thine.
Take, O take the gift and giver.
Take and serve thyself with me,
Alabama, Alabama,
I will aye be true to thee.

FAMOUS PEOPLE

Aaron, Hank (1934–), baseball player

Carver, George Washington (1864–1943), scientist, botanist

Cole, Nat "King" (1919–1965), singer

Davis, Jefferson (1808–1889), president of the Confederate States of America

Fitzgerald, Zelda (1900–1948), author

Handy, W. C. (1873–1958), musician and composer

Harris, Emmylou (1947–), country singer

Keller, Helen (1880–1968), author and lecturer

King, Martin Luther, Jr. (1929–1968), civil rights activist and clergyman

Lee, Harper (1926–), author

Lewis, Carl (1961–), track athlete

Louis, Joe (1914–1981), boxer

Mays, Willie (1931–), baseball player

Parks, Rosa (1913–), civil rights activist

Red Eagle (William Weatherford) (ca. 1780–1824), American Indian leader

Rice, Condoleezza (1954–), U.S. Secretary of State

Taylor, Mildred D. (1943–), children's author

Washington, Booker T. (1856–1915), educator

Wallace, George (1919–1998), governor

Williams, Hank (1923–1953), country singer

TO FIND OUT MORE

At the Library

Crane, Carol, and Ted Burn (illustrator). *Y Is for Yellowhammer: An Alabama Alphabet*. Chelsea, Mich.: Sleeping Bear Press, 2003.

Feeney, Kathy. *Alabama*. New York: Children's Press, 2002.

King, Martin Luther, Jr. *I Have a Dream*. New York: Scholastic Press, 1997.

Lundell, Margo, and Irene Trivas (illustrator). *A Girl Named Helen Keller*. New York: Scholastic, 1995.

On the Web

Visit our home page for lots of links about Alabama:
http://www.childsworld.com/links

Note to Parents, Teachers, and Librarians: We routinely verify our Web links to make sure they are safe, active sites—so encourage your readers to check them out!

Places to Visit or Contact

Alabama Bureau of Tourism & Travel
401 Adams Avenue, Suite 126
PO Box 4927
Montgomery, AL 36103-4927
334/242-4169
For more information about traveling in Alabama

Alabama Department of Archives and History
624 Washington Avenue
Montgomery, AL 36130-0100
334/242-4435
For more information about the history of Alabama

INDEX

Bye, Heart of Dixie.
We had a great time.
We'll come back soon!